Sometimes Jokes Aren't Funny

What to Do About Hidden Bullying

by Amanda F. Doering

pictures by Simone Shin

PICTURE WINDOW BOOKS
a capstone imprint

Note to Parents and Educators

Bullying has serious, long-term consequences for both the person who is bullied and the person who bullies. Bullying should not be considered part of growing up. For bullying to stop, adults and children need to learn to recognize bullying behavior, and develop immediate and fair ways of dealing with it.

Recognizing hidden bullying isn't always easy. Hidden bullying is often about power within relationships or groups of friends. Ignoring a peer, purposefully excluding someone from groups, hurtful jokes, and public embarrassment are examples of hidden bullying.

While reading this book, encourage the child to talk about his or her own experiences with hidden bullying. Has the child experienced hidden bullying, witnessed someone being bullied, or acted as a bully? What did the child do in these situations? Did he or she handle the situations correctly?

Thanks to our adviser for her expertise, research, and advice:
Dorothy L. Espelage, PhD
Department of Educational Psychology
University of Illinois, Urbana-Champaign

Editor: Michelle Hasselius
Designer: Lori Bye
Creative Director: Nathan Gassman
Production Specialist: Laura Manthe
The illustrations in this book were created digitally.

Picture Window Books are published by Capstone,
1710 Roe Crest Drive, North Mankato, Minnesota 56003
www.capstonepub.com

Copyright © 2016 by Picture Window Books, a Capstone imprint. All rights reserved. No part of this publication may be reproduced in whole or in part, or stored in a retrieval system, or transmitted in any form or by any means, electronic, mechanical, photocopying, recording, or otherwise, without written permission of the publisher.

Design elements: Shutterstock:JungleOutThere

Library of Congress Cataloging-in-Publication Data
Doering, Amanda F., 1980–
Sometimes jokes aren't funny : what to do about hidden bullying / by Amanda F. Doering.
pages cm
Audience: K to Grade 3.
Summary: "Sensitive, narrative text from illustrated animal characters shows readers what covert bullying is and provides possible solutions to stop it"—Provided by publisher.
ISBN 978-1-4795-6943-4 (library binding)
ISBN 978-1-4795-6959-5 (paperback)
ISBN 978-1-4795-6963-2 (eBook PDF)
1. Bullying—Juvenile literature. 2. Bullying—Prevention—Juvenile literature. I. Title.
BF637.B85T687 2016
302.34'3—dc23   2014049226

Every summer Terry, Sydney, and I go to Camp Barkley. I was really excited this year, because we're all in the same cabin. But then a new kid named Taylor showed up to stay with us.

Taylor makes jokes and acts cool. But Taylor's jokes aren't always funny. Sometimes they're just mean.

Yesterday I told Taylor I sell candy and magazines to pay for camp. Taylor told everyone at our lunch table I had to sell candy because I'm poor.

Some of the kids giggled. I felt my cheeks turn bright red. I left the table.

"Just kidding!" Taylor called after me, laughing.

After dinner Taylor pulled Terry and Sydney aside and whispered something to them. Soon they headed my way.

"Jamie, Taylor is going to buy us ice-cream cones at the camp store," said Sydney. "Wanna come?"

"Actually, I don't have enough money for four cones," said Taylor. "So if you want to come, Jamie, you'll have to pay for your own."

Taylor paused for a second. "Oh, but you probably can't afford ice cream because you're poor." Taylor shrugged. "Sorry!"

The three of them left, and I was alone.

A person doesn't need to hit or call someone names to be a bully. Sometimes a bully will leave someone out of an activity on purpose. He or she will encourage others in the group to exclude the person too.

Later, Terry, Sydney, and Taylor walked into the cabin with their ice-cream cones. They were whispering and laughing.

I was trying to read, but I felt ashamed and angry. Terry and Sydney are *my* friends. Why was Taylor picking on me?

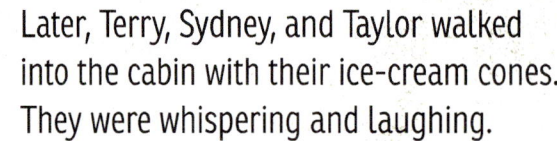

The three sat on Taylor's bunk. "Jamie, come and join us!" Terry called.

"Yeah, Jamie," said Taylor. "Come tell us more stories about being poor."

I turned toward the wall, pretending to read. Then I started to cry. I couldn't help it.

"Jeez, I was just kidding!" Taylor acted upset. "Learn how to take a joke."

Sometimes jokes can be fun. But they can go too far. If jokes or teasing make you sad or angry, it's OK to tell the other person to stop.

Today we're writing postcards to our parents. But Terry, Sydney, and Taylor are laughing and whispering instead of writing.

Suddenly they get very quiet. I look over and see Sydney give me a dirty look. Terry looks ready to cry. Taylor is smirking. I ask Sydney and Terry what's wrong, but they both ignore me.

"You know," says Taylor, "you shouldn't say that Terry smells bad."

The three of them get up and walk away before I can say anything.
I never said Terry smelled bad!

Some bullies will gossip or spread rumors. By telling lies or embarrassing stories, they can get other kids to dislike or bully the person too.

Tonight at the campfire, Sydney and Terry pretend I'm not here. I'm sitting right next to them!

They talk about the big camping trip we get to go on at the end of the week.

"We're staying in three-person tents," says Taylor. "You and Terry will stay with me." Sydney nods in agreement.

"But what about Jamie?" I hear Terry whisper to Sydney.

Taylor's eyes roll. "Come on, Terry," Taylor says. "You don't want to be friends with someone who says mean things about you."

"Mean things?" I ask loudly. "I never said you smelled, Terry!"

They still pretend I'm not here. I feel so sad and frustrated. I give up and leave.

In the morning, I sit by myself at breakfast. I find an empty table at lunch too.

I feel so alone.

Back at my cabin, I see a group of kids gathered around the front door. When they see me, some kids giggle. Others walk away with their heads down.

There on the door is a photo of me during our first year of camp. I'm holding my favorite stuffed bear and sucking my thumb. Someone has written **"baby bed wetter"** on the photo.

I run away from the cabin as fast as I can.

Terry finds me. "What do you want?" I mumble.

"I want to say I'm sorry," says Terry. "I should have stood up for you. I wasn't being a good friend. I was afraid if I did, Taylor would make fun of me too."

"I didn't say you smelled bad," I say. "I would never tell people mean things about you."

"I know that now," says Terry, smiling sadly.

People who watch and see bullying are called bystanders. Bystanders can help stop bullying by sticking up for others. If you see someone being bullied, tell the bully to stop or ask an adult for help.

Terry and I walk back toward camp. We're surprised to see Sydney shouting at Taylor.

"I can't believe you stole that photo from me!" Sydney yells. "I should have never shown it to you."

"Hey, lay off!" Taylor laughs. "It was just a joke."

"Sometimes your jokes aren't funny, Taylor. Sometimes they're just mean!" Sydney says.

Sydney walks over to us. "I'm really sorry about the photo, Jamie," Sydney says. "I hope we can still be friends."

Sydney thinks we should talk to an adult about what Taylor has said and done. We tell our camp counselor, Jean, about how mean Taylor has been. Jean listens to us.

"I'm glad you came to me," Jean says. "Joking around with friends can be fun. But sometimes joking goes too far, and friends get hurt. Some people use jokes as an excuse to say hurtful things, and that's not OK. Mean jokes and spreading rumors to hurt or embarrass someone is bullying."

I hadn't thought of it that way. But it makes sense. I feel a lot better after talking to Jean.

It's good to stand up for yourself and others. But you shouldn't try to handle bullying alone. It's always best to tell an adult you trust. The adult can stop the bullying behavior and get everyone the help he or she needs.

Jean moves Taylor to a different cabin. I don't see Taylor much after that, which is fine with me. Terry and Sydney stay away from Taylor too.

As punishment for bullying, Taylor isn't allowed to go on the camping trip. Terry, Sydney, and I have a great time.

It wasn't the perfect summer, but the end of camp was fun. And we all learned a good lesson. Sometimes jokes aren't funny.

Glossary

ashamed—feeling shame, guilt, or embarrassment

bully—to frighten or pick on someone over and over

bunk—a narrow bed

bystander—a person who watches something but doesn't take part

cabin—a small house, often built of wood

counselor—a person trained to help people with problems or give advice

frustrated—to be upset about something

gossip—to talk about other people, often in a false or unkind way

rumor—something said by many people; a rumor may not be true

smirk—to smile in an unpleasant way because you are pleased with yourself or glad about someone else's trouble

threaten—to say you will harm someone or something in the future

verbal—spoken or made up of words

Read More

Ferguson, Addy. *Group Bullying: Exclusion and Ganging Up.* Stand Up: Bullying Prevention. New York: PowerKids Press, 2013.

Higgins, Melissa. *I Am Caring.* I Don't Bully. North Mankato, Minn.: Capstone Press, 2014.

Mull, Brandon. *Pingo and the Playground Bully.* Salt Lake City, Utah: Shadow Mountain, 2012.

Internet Sites

FactHound offers a safe, fun way to find Internet sites related to this book. All of the sites on FactHound have been researched by our staff.

Here's all you do:

Visit *www.facthound.com*

Type in this code: 9781479569434

Index

bystanders, 4, 15, 16

counselors, 21, 22

crying, 9, 10

feelings, 3, 8, 9, 13, 14, 16, 21

friends, 8, 13, 16, 19, 21

hidden bullying
    types of, 4, 5, 6, 7, 9, 10, 11, 12, 13, 15, 19
    ways to stop, 9, 16, 21

joking
    fun versus mean, 3, 9, 19, 21

laughing, 5, 8, 10

talking to adults, 16, 21

whispering, 6, 8, 10, 13

All of the books in the series:

  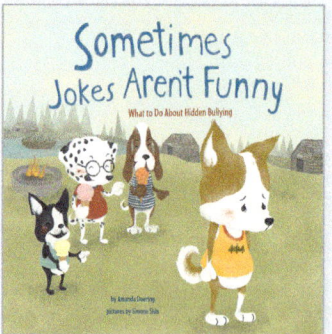 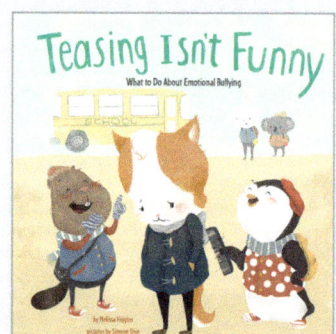